THE UNDERTAKER'S DAUGHTER

PITT POETRY SERIES
Ed Ochester, Editor

The Undertaker's Daughter

TOI DERRICOTTE

University of Pittsburgh Press

Published by the University of Pittsburgh Press, Pittsburgh, PA 15260

Manufactured in the United States of America

Printed on acid-free paper

10 9 8 7 6 5 4 3 2 1

ISBN 13: 978-0-8229-6200-7

ISBN 10: 0-8229-6200-4

For Tony, Cami, and Elliot

The dreadful war nature wages
to prevent the Poet from existing.

—George Seferis, *Days of 1945–1951*

CONTENTS

PART I

The Undertaker's Daughter

I am not afraid to be memoir

*Before the amphetamine of accomplishment; when there was only a
physical body and a mind circulating through it like blood, with hardly
a hovering angel, chunky, spirited, too big for her britches, on the
two-wheeler before the grown-ups rose, driving the neighbors crazy on
Sunday morning when the neighborhood should be quiet, first tendency
to test, legs and eyes, standing up on the seat with one leg out behind her,
one or two hands on the handlebars, like a circus lady riding bareback,
back to loneliness, back back before angels separated and became the
mad god.*

*I want to go back there, without a platform except that rising of the
body itself, that challenge up to being, I want to go back to where the
first and last wisdom forms, the secret self locked in the tentative field
of protoplasm, whatever was cooled and cooked on the rock, whatever
mitochondria god stuck his thumb in, back back, I am not afraid to be
memoir.*

Burial sites

Trauma is not what happens to us, but what we hold inside us in the absence of an empathetic witness.
—Peter Levine, *The Unspoken Voice*

I.

The first was a bassinet. I don't remember what it was made of; I think it was one of those big white wicker baskets with wheels. When I couldn't sleep at night, my father would drag it into the kitchen. It was winter. He'd light the gas oven. I remember the room's stuffiness, the acrid bite of cold and fumes.

My father didn't like crying. He said I was doing it to get attention. He didn't like my mother teaching me that I could cry and get attention. Nothing was wrong with me, and, even if I was hungry, it wasn't time to eat. Sometimes, I screamed for hours, and my father—I do remember this—would push his chair up to the lip of the bassinet and smoke, as if he were keeping me company.

After a few nights, he had broken me. I stopped crying. But, when he put the bottle to my lips, I was too exhausted to drink.

II.

My second was a crib in the corner of my parents' room. We moved to the attic when I was eighteen months old, so it must have been before that. I still didn't sleep at night. I'd see a huge gray monster outside the window, swaying toward me and side to side. I was afraid that, any moment, it would swoop in and get me. But I couldn't wake my parents. What if it wasn't real but only the huge blue spruce outside the window? If I woke them for nothing my father would be angry. I was more afraid of my father than I was of the monster. If I just kept watching, it couldn't get me.

III.

My aunt brought home a present for me every day when she came from work. I'd wait by the kitchen door as soon as I could walk. Sometimes, she'd fish down in her pocketbook, and the only thing she could find was a Tums, which she called candy. But mostly she'd bring colored paper and pencils from the printing press where she worked.

When I was two or three, I began to draw things and to write my name. I wrote it backward for a long time: "I-O-T." I drew houses, cars, money, and animals. I actually believed everything I drew was real; the house was a real house, as real as the one we lived in. I held it in my hand. It belonged to me, like a chair or an apple. From then on, I did not understand my mother's sadness or my father's rage. If we could have whatever we wanted just by drawing it, there was nothing to miss or to long for. I tried to show them what I meant, but they shrugged it off, not seeing or believing.

(This sideways escape—the battle between my father's worst thought of me and this proof, this stream of something, questioned and found lacking, which must remain nearly invisible—pressed into what leaks out as involuntarily as urine, a message which must be passed over the coals, raked, purified into a thin strand of unambiguous essence of the deep core.)

IV.

When I was seven, we moved to the Forest Lodge. We lived in D12 on the fourth floor. My mother and father slept in the living room on a bed that came down out of the wall. I slept on a rollaway cot kept in the same closet and pulled out at night. I helped my mother roll it into a corner of the kitchen, push the kitchen table back and open the cot, its sheets and blankets still tight. (Whatever I had, I kept nice. I had to. My bed was my bed, but it was in my mother's space. If she needed the space, my bed would go.)

Someone had given me an easel-shaped blackboard with a sheet of clear plastic that you could pull down and paint on. In the morning, my mother would set it up in a small area between the dining room and the kitchen. She didn't mind if the colors spilled, if a few drops fell on the newsprint she had put down. After she scrubbed every Saturday, she liked to put newspaper over the linoleum to keep it clean of our footprints. Wednesday, halfway through the week, she'd take the torn, dirty papers up, and, underneath, the floor was like new.

V.

Most times I liked my food. I didn't mind eating until my daddy started making me clean my plate and either struck me off my chair if I didn't or lifted me up by my hair and held me midair if I was slow. He wanted me to eat faster; he didn't have all day.

He'd hold me off the floor until I pleaded. I'd sputter in fear and humiliation—I don't remember pain—but I had to button up before he put me down to do exactly what he had told me to do, fast.

Slowness was a sign of insubordination. If I missed a pea or a crumb, I was trying to outwit him. I must have thought he was stupid. And if I pleaded that I hadn't seen the pea, he'd know I was lying. "Your story is so touching till it sounds like a lie."

I swallowed it down; I wiped that look off my face. But still he would notice my bottom lip beginning to quiver. This was a personal insult, as if I had taken a knife and put it to his face. If my brow wrinkled in a question—"Do you love me, daddy? How could you hurt me like this?"—this implied I was pursuing my own version of the truth, as if I were his victim.

It was a war of wills, as he so clearly saw, and these were my attempts to subvert him, to make my will reign, to plant my flag.

He was the ruler of my body. I had to learn that. He had to be deep in me, deeper than instinct, like the commander of a submarine during times of war.

VI.

Thinking was the thing about me that most offended or hurt him, the thing he most wanted to kill. Just in case my mind might be heading in that direction, here was a stop sign, a warning: "Who do you think you are?" But the words weren't enough. They'd bubble out of him like some brew exploding from an escape hatch, a vortex that pulled in his whole body, his huge hands, which grabbed me up by my hair.

Where could I go? I was trapped in what my father thought I was thinking. I couldn't think. My thinking disappeared in case it was the wrong thought.

It was not the world that I needed to take in, but my father's voice. I had to see exactly what my father saw in me—and stay out of its way.

VII.

In the morning, I'd fold up my bed and put it away. On those days and nights when my father didn't come home, we didn't need the space in the kitchen for breakfast or dinner, so we didn't put my bed away. I'd make it without a wrinkle, the pillow placed carefully on top, and it would stay in the little space under the window.

Maybe the black phone had rung saying he'd be late. Or maybe she had put him out.

I didn't know how they slept in the same bed because they never touched. Once, I saw them kiss. Maybe it was her birthday or Mother's Day. They blushed when they saw I saw them.

VIII.

> *Those caught in such a vicious abuse-reactive cycle will not only continue to expose the animals they love to suffering merely to prove that they themselves can no longer be hurt, but they are also given to testing the boundaries of their own desensitization through various acts of self-mutilation. In short, such children can only achieve a sense of safety and empowerment by inflicting pain and suffering on themselves and others.*
> —"The Animal-Cruelty Syndrome," *New York Times Magazine*, June 13, 2010

I am trying to get as close as possible to the place in me where the change occurred: I had to take that voice in, become my father, the

7

judge referred to before any dangerous self-assertion, any thought or feeling. I happened in reverse: my body took in the pummeling actions, which went down into my core. I ask myself first, before any love or joy or passion, anything that might grow from me: "Who do you think you are?" I suppress the possibilities.

IX.

My mother used the small inheritance she received from her mother to put my father through embalming school. He moved to Chicago for the few months of training at Worsham, the college for black undertakers. She hoped to raise us up—her mother had been a cook— to become an undertaker's wife, one of the highest positions of black society. But when he came back from the school, my father wouldn't take the mean $5 a week his stepfather offered him to apprentice. He wouldn't swallow his pride. He also wouldn't take jobs offered by his stepfather's competitors. That, too, was a matter of pride, not to sell out the family name.

My father never did practice undertaking for a living. Though, sometimes, when I was young, friends would ask him to embalm someone they loved and my father would acquiesce. He would enter the embalming room at Webster's Funeral Home, put on the robe, take up the tools, and his stepfather would step back. His reputation grew in this way. People who saw the bodies he had worked on—especially the body of the beautiful and wealthy Elsie Roxborough, who died by her own hand and was buried in a head-to-foot glass casket like Sleeping Beauty—marveled at his art and agreed he had the best touch of anyone.

People praised him for conducting the most elegant service; for knowing exactly what to say to comfort the bereaved, for holding their arms and escorting them to the first funeral car, for convincing those who needed to cry that it was all right; yet knowing too how to quiet them so there were no embarrassing "shows."

My father knew the workings of the heart; that's why so many

8

people—my grandmother; his stepfather; and even his best friend Rad, whose heart he had crushed—loved him even after he let them down completely and many times, even after he abandoned them or did the meanest things. My father was with each of them, holding their hands, when they died. My handsome, charming father, the ultimate lover, the ultimate knower of the heart.

X.

My father knew all about the body. He had learned in embalming school. For a while after his mother died, he stopped smoking and drinking and came home at night. He'd get out the huge leather-bound dictionary (*Webster*'s—the same as our last name!) that my grandmother had given him when he graduated. He would open it to a picture of the bones in the middle of the book, which had three see-through overlays: on the first, the blue muscles; on the second, the red blood vessels; and, finally, on the third, the white nerves.

He loved the body, loved knowing how things worked. He taught me the longest name of a muscle, the sternocleidomastoid, a cradle or hammock that was strung between the sternum and mastoid. He'd amaze me with long, multisyllabic words; then he'd test me on the spelling.

My father always explained. He always showed me the little smear on the plate that I had set to drain before he'd make me do all the dishes over again. He'd explain how he had studied hard so he knew where to hit me and not leave a single mark. He'd brag about it. He wanted me to appreciate the quality of his work. Like any good teacher, he wanted to pass it down.

XI.

During the summer when my mother and aunt were cleaning and wanted me out of the house, I would go out to the side of the house with a flyswatter and command the flies not to land on my wall. There were hundreds of flies, and though I told them not to, they continued to land. I don't think I said it out loud. I think I said it—screamed it, really—in my mind. Sometimes, I believed that the things in the world heard your thoughts, the way God heard your prayers. When I was very young, not even out of my crib, I'd ask the shades to blow a certain way to prove they had heard me.

The flies were disobeying me. Whenever one landed, I would go after it with the flyswatter. I was furious that they would do what I had commanded them not to. I knew they understood, or would understand finally. I killed tens, hundreds—didn't they see? —but they wouldn't stop.

I knew I was murderous, and yet, was it murder to kill flies? My aunt and mother never stopped me.

XII.

Before my grandmother died when I was ten, she had three dogs. Each had a short life. Patsy was the "good" dog who died of a chicken bone in her stomach, and Smokey was the "bad" dog who growled at people and would jump over the second-story banister on the porch and walk around on the outside of the rail. When my grandmother and grandfather were downstairs in the undertaking parlor, they would leave me alone with Smokey. I was about seven and I had learned the voice the nuns used to say cruel things to the children who were slow. Sometimes, the nuns hit those children over the knuckles with a ruler, but mostly they just humiliated them, made them sit in the back and never called on them to do errands. I tried to teach Smokey to stay behind the gate to the pantry. I would open the gate and tell him to stay, and when he went out in the kitchen, I'd hit him with his leash. I believe I hit him hard, maybe as hard as my father hit me. I wanted to feel that power.

I did this two, three, or four times and, though it seems impossible that my grandparents didn't know, no one stopped me. One time I came over, and my grandmother said Smokey had run away, jumped over the second-story banister to the street and didn't die. He was never seen again. Was he that desperate to get away? I felt sad and responsible. I felt glad.

XIII.

I was nine when we moved to a bigger apartment on the first floor. Now, my father had only one flight to carry me up by my hair. He didn't mind going public—the stairs were right in the lobby—but he refused to allow me to scream in terror when he grabbed me. Not because he was afraid people would see. My screaming made him furious because I knew he was only going to carry me up the stairs and scream at me, only beat me on the thighs and calves (where it wouldn't show), and only until I made every look of pain, confusion, and fury disappear. He knew I knew that. So what was all that broadcasting, as if something really bad was going to happen, as if he was going to kill me?

XIV.

Life is something you have to get used to: what is normal in a house, the bottom line, what is taken for granted. I always had good food. Our house was clean. My mother was tired and sad most of the time. My mother spent most of her day cleaning.

We had a kitchen with a little dining space, a living room, a bedroom, a bathroom and two halls, one that led to the bathroom and the bedroom, and one that led to the front door. There was a linen closet in the hall between the bedroom and the bathroom. My books and toys all went into a drawer that I had to straighten every Saturday. There was a closet in the bedroom for my mother's clothes, a closet in the front hall for my father's, and a closet off the living room that held my mother's bed.

It was a huge metal apparatus that somehow swept out on a hinge. I can't imagine how my mother and I, as small as we were, brought it out and put it back every night and every morning, for my father was hardy ever there. We just grabbed on, exerted a little force, and pulled it straight toward us. It seemed to glide by itself, swinging outward around the corner; then it would stand up, rocking, balancing, until we pulled it down.

XV.

My father and I shared the small bedroom, and my mother slept on the pullout in the living room so that she wouldn't wake us when she got dressed in the morning to go to her new job. We slept in twin beds she had bought us, pushed up close together.

I had special things given to me, special things she paid for: the expensive toys I got for Christmas that took a whole year to pay for and the clothes I wore from Himelhoch's while my mother wore an old plaid coat for eleven years. Now I was a big girl moving from a little cot in the kitchen to my own bed in a bedroom. My father and I always got the best.

XVI.

My mother shopped after work every Thursday, so my father would come home and fix dinner for me. He'd stop at Fadell's Market and get a big steak with a bone in it. He'd bring it home and unwrap the brown paper, slowly, savoring one corner at a time, like someone doing a striptease or opening a trove of stolen diamonds. He'd brag about how much money he had spent. He'd broil it right up next to the flame, spattering grease, fire, and smoke, only a couple of minutes on each side, cooked still bloody, nearly raw, the way we liked it, he said—different from my mother. He'd say he liked it just knocked over the head with a hammer and dragged over a hot skillet. His eyebrows would go wild, and he'd rub his hands together like a fly.

XVII.

Once, my father took me to the movies. We walked downtown to the Fox Theater on one unusually warm Thursday evening during my Christmas vacation to see Bing Crosby in *The Bells of St. Mary*. My father frequently promised things he didn't deliver, like the time he promised to come home and pray the family rosary every night for a week when I carried the huge statue of The Virgin home in a box as big as a violin case. He never came home once. When I turned The Virgin back in at school, I had to lie to the nun. After that, I rarely asked for anything. But going to the movies was his idea.

I was never happier than when I was with my father and he was in a good mood. He liked to tease me and make me laugh. He was so handsome that I felt proud when people noticed us. I thought they were thinking that my father really enjoyed me, that I was a very special girl. I acted like a special girl, happy and pretty, until I almost believed it. I had dressed up, and we stopped for a Coney Island and caramel corn, which were his favorites.

XVIII.

By this time, my father didn't come home most nights. Sometimes, he and my mother wouldn't speak to each other for months. Sometimes, they wouldn't speak even to me when we were in the house together, as if we had to be quiet, like in church, and respect their hatred for each other.

My father thought I hated him like my mother did or else he didn't think I was worth talking to, for he'd often go months without speaking even when we were in the house alone.

I tried to make him change. I'd make up special names like "D-dats." "Hi D-dats," I'd meet him at the door when he came home at night. I knew he liked to feel young and hip. I'd make my voice happy, as if I weren't afraid he'd find a shoe or book out of place and beat me. I actually was happy when I was with him—I had to be! He could see inside me. He could tell my moods. My unhappiness blamed him.

Maybe all that silence and beating was because he thought nobody loved him, not my mother and not his mother. He told me how his mother had knocked him down when he was a grown man. He told me how my mother always picked up his ashtrays to wash them as soon as he put his cigarette out. I tried to make him feel loved. Sometimes, we played "Step on a crack you break your mother's back" when we were coming home from his mother's house, as if the two of us were in cahoots.

XIX.

Once, when I was ten or eleven, he came home for lunch, and I asked him if I could dance for him. I had seen Rita Hayworth dance the Dance of the Seven Veils. I had stayed home sick and practiced. I liked to dance on the bed so I could see myself in my mother's dressing table mirror.

I wore old see-through curtains and my mother's jewelry on my head like a crown. I must have had something underneath for I knew some things mustn't show. I thought, maybe, if he saw I was almost a woman and could do what beautiful women do, he might find a reason to love me.

At the end, I spun around and around until most of the drapes, towels, and my mother's nightgown fell to the floor. I don't remember what remained to cover me.

XX.

Sometimes, on the nights he came home, I'd sneak up on him while he was reading the newspaper and pull off his slipper.

He'd put the paper down very deliberately, put on his "mean" play-face and say, "Oh, you want to play, huh?" And he'd grab me up like an ogre. He'd hold me down and jab his fingers into my ribs.

"No," I'd scream, "I'm sorry," and I'd plead that I would pee if he didn't let me up.

Finally, he'd relent. "You're not going to do it again?" And he'd tickle me more.

"Never, never," I'd scream.

"Are you sure?"

As soon as he picked up the paper again and seemed to turn his attention away, I'd go back.

My father could make me laugh. He knew just where to hit the funny bone. Always, my father was the only one who could make me swallow pills or sit still while he administered burning iodine. When I fell or took the wrong step over a picket fence, I'd come to him, crying. "I'm going to have a big scar and nobody will love me." And he'd tease, "Oh, my poor little baby, all the boys are going to call her 'old scar leg,' and she's going to be alone for the rest of her life"; but he'd do what had to be done, hold the leg in place, put the iodine on the raw spot, right where it was needed, direct and quick, without flinching, never afraid to cause the necessary pain.

XXI.

On Saturday mornings, my mother and I would have toast and coffee in her bed. She let me lie there while she planned our day. She'd get up barefoot and put the coffee on and make me sugar toast. I loved those Saturday mornings near her: her big bed, her cold cream smell.

I had always thought my mother was frightened of my father. She never seemed to fight straight. She got him by going the back route, like the look on her face when she got in the orange and yellow truck that he bought when he started the egg business. She sat on the orange crate—he called it the passenger seat—and never laughed, never joined in on the fun as he took us around Belle Isle. He had been so happy when he jingled the keys, but you could tell she thought that old truck was nothing to be proud of, as if even a joke about such a poor thing was in bad taste.

Then one Saturday morning, I spotted a big roach, a water-bug, on the living room floor. I jumped up on the bed and started screaming; she came from the kitchen, grabbed her house shoe and got down on all fours. The thing charged her from under the chair like a warrior. I was screaming like crazy. I realized she was my last protection. And she started punching at the thing, punching the floor, anywhere she could punch. She didn't stop until it was flattened.

I had never seen my mother brave. I had never seen that she would fight to the death. It was a part of her she never showed. I had thought she didn't stop my father from beating me because she was afraid. I was confused by her braveness.

XXII.

My mother was sad. She didn't feel appreciated. I didn't do enough to help. She hurt inside. Her body suffered. Her feet swelled black with poison. She had a dead baby. She had womb problems. They had to take the knotted thing out. The doctor rubbed her stomach for hours until she went to the bathroom. She got TB. She got a goiter. She shouldn't clean so hard; she should rest, at least late in the afternoon. But she wouldn't. She had to keep doing what hurt her.

My mother and father were at war; whoever loved the other first would lose.

XXIII.

Nobody thought the little marks were worth looking at. I cried and showed how they went up my arm all the way to my elbow, ran all over my ankles and the tops of my feet, even up my thighs. I could see them, but when anyone else looked, the marks disappeared.

Maybe they didn't itch. Maybe they weren't serious. Maybe I was causing trouble. (I had an active imagination, my mother and father said.) I couldn't sleep because something was happening in my bed—a misery—and everybody acted as if it wasn't. It didn't hurt after a while. I could take my mind off it and put it somewhere else.

I think the only reason my mother finally believed me was because I kept showing her that Monday mornings, after I had spent the weekend with my aunt, I didn't have the marks, but Tuesdays, after I had slept in my own bed, I had the marks again.

In an instant of recognition, she raced into the bedroom, flipped my covers off the bed and saw the little bits of blood. She turned over the mattress, and there, in the corners, were the nests of a thousand bedbugs, lethargic or crawling. She looked close. They had gotten so far inside that the room had to be sealed with tape, a bomb put in.

He had been sleeping with another woman. He had brought her dirt into his own home (though he said the bugs came in egg crates).

Bedbugs were what poor women had, women who couldn't do better, women who didn't matter. Some other woman's bedbugs were making my mother the same as that woman.

He had brought in everything she hated, everything she couldn't control: the helplessness of slavery, bad births, poverty, illness, death. Everything she had risked her life to clean out of our apartment.

My mother had reason for outrage.

I only had reason to itch.

XXIV.

The living room was off limits. There was too much that might get messed up or broken. I guess he chose rooms to beat me in honor of the sacrifices my mother had made to make our home beautiful.

In the bedroom, where could I go when I fell? I wouldn't fall on the wooden footboards. There was an aisle between my mother's closet and my father's bed. That was too narrow. On the left side of the doorway was my mother's dressing table, where I'd sit and put on necklaces, earrings, and nail polish and look in the mirror. There wasn't room for me to flail around, so my father had to be very specific about the direction in which his blows would aim me.

If my cousin was visiting, he would inform her, his voice sincere but matter-of-fact—"I'm going to have to take Toi to the bathroom." He preferred the bathroom when she was visiting, except when my mother was in on it, and then we needed a bigger space. If, for example, my mother had told him I talked back, he'd say, "We're going to have to speak to Toi in the kitchen." He'd pull me by my arm and close the kitchen door, which had glass panes so that my cousin could see.

But she said she averted her eyes, knowing it would humiliate me. She remembers him sliding off his belt; she remembers me pleading each time the belt hit; she remembers him telling me, as he was beating me, in rhythm, why he was doing it and what I shouldn't do the next time. I would come out, trying not to show how I had been afraid for my life, how I had pleaded without pride. I thought those things would have made her hate me.

*

I remember the hitting, but not the feeling of the hits; I remember falling and trying to cover my legs with my hands.

I remember the time I came home with a migraine and begged him not to beat me. "Please, please, daddy, it hurts so bad." I could hardly speak. I had to walk level, my head a huge cup of water that might spill on the floor.

Why couldn't he see my pain? My head seemed to be splitting open, my eyes bleeding. I didn't know what might happen if I tipped my head even slightly. He saw me walking like that, as if someone had placed delicate glass statues on my arms and shoulders. I begged him, *not now.* I knew I had it coming. I had gone out with the Childs, and he had left a note telling me not to go out.

*

The Childs lived on the fourth floor. Sometimes, they brought down the best rice with butter and just the right amount of salt and pepper. They had no children. They had a little bubble-shaped car. We all seemed glad to roll the windows down and go out to their niece's. She turned her bike over to me. It was so much fun pumping it up and down the hill, letting my hair fly. I forgot my father, as I had forgotten the bug bites, as I forgot what it felt like to be beaten. I just thought, *I'm pumping harder so I will go faster and let the air hit my face and arms, and then I'll stop pumping at the top and fall down and down, my feet up off the pedals.* And I didn't feel fat: My body lost weight—it just went with everything going in that direction, and the wind flew against me in the other direction. Though it blew in my face and began to sting, I

18

couldn't stop pumping, couldn't stop trying, one more time, to bring myself to that moment of pleasure and accomplishment right before I'd let go.

I had never felt such power, earning it by my own work and skill. I could ride it. I was the girl in charge; I had the power to bring myself there.

XXV.

Shortly after I was married, we had a dog that kept shitting on the floor. Once, I took a coat hanger and was going to hit her with it, but she drew back her lips and snarled at me in self-defense and fury. I had no idea that she would defend herself. I was shocked. I thought she was going to attack me, and I put the hanger down. I respected her in a different way after that.

She lived for sixteen years and was a great mothering presence in our household. It seemed every dog and cat that came in the house had to lie beside her, with some part of its body—a paw, the hind— touching hers. Once, I heard a strange noise during the night and went to investigate. A kitten my son had found on the railroad tracks was nursing from her, and she was sleeping, as if she just expected to be a mother. When I would come home, after I had been away for a while, she'd jump up on the bed and curl her butt into my belly, and I'd put my arms around her and hold her like a lover. When she died, I missed her so much I realized that she had been my mother, too. She taught me it was beautiful to defend yourself—and that you could be unafraid of touch.

*

I remember how, occasionally, my father's dogs would pull back and snarl at him when he was viciously beating them. His anger would increase immeasurably. They had truly given him a reason to kill them. "You think you can get away with that in my house?" he'd ask, the same as he'd ask me.

Once, to get away from him, one of his dogs leapt through the glass storm door in the kitchen and ran down 14th Street bleeding to death.

XXVI.

You would think that the one treated so cruelly would "kill" the abuser, throw him out of the brain forever. What a horrific irony that the abuser is the one most taken in, most remembered; the imprint of those who were loving and kind is secondary, like a passing cloud. Sometimes, I thought that's why my father beat me. Because he was afraid he would be forgotten. And he achieved what he wanted.

In the deepest place of judgment, not critical thinking, not on that high plain, but judgment of first waking, judgment of the sort that decides what inner face to turn toward the morning—in that first choosing moment of what to say to myself, the place from which first language blossoms—I choose, must choose, my father's words.

The twisted snarl of his unbelief turned everything good into something undeserved, so that nothing convinces enough—no man or woman or child, no play or work or art. There is no inner loyalty, no way of belonging. I cannot trust what I feel and connect to; I cannot love or hold anything in my hand, any fragile thing—a living blue egg, my own baby—in the same way that I never convinced my father I was his. And I must rest on it, as on bedrock.

XXVII.

The time I had the migraine, after my father had beaten me, he made me bathe. He drew the bath, felt the water with his fingers and made sure it wouldn't burn. He told me to go in there and take off my clothes.

The water, when I put my toe in, was like walking in fire. I stood there, holding myself.

And then—instead of letting my father kill me or bashing my own head against the tile to end all knowing—I crouched down, letting the lukewarm water touch me.

Oh, water, how can you hurt me this bad? What did I do to you? I was whimpering. I don't know if I still had hope he would hear me, or if I just couldn't stop the sound from leaking out of my body.

But my father came and lifted me out of the water in his arms, took me naked, laid me on my bed and covered me lightly with a sheet. Then he went away and left me in the dark as if to cool down, and he brought cut lemon slices for my eyes and a cool towel or pads of alcohol to put on my forehead. He bathed me in tenderness, as if he really knew I was suffering and he wanted me to feel better.

I wondered if he finally believed. If he realized from within himself that I had been telling the truth, that I wasn't evil. Maybe he had some idea of how much he had hurt me. I knew that, sometimes, men beat their women and then make up. I didn't know which daddy was real.

Afterword:

I hear in myself a slight opposition, a wounded presence saying, I am me, I know who I am. But I am left with only a narrow hole, a thin tube of rubber that the words must squeak through. Where words might have gushed out as from a struck well, now, instead, I watch it—watch every thought. It wasn't my father's thought that I took in; it was his language. It is the language in me that must change.

The undertaker's daughter

Terrified at a reading to read
poems about my fears & shames,

a voice in me said: *Just
open your mouth.* Now

I read about Anubis, the God of Egypt

who ushered the dead
to the underworld, who performed the ritual of

the opening of the mouth

so they could
see, hear & eat.

Had it been my father speaking,

giving me back that
depth of taste & color,

fineness of sound
that his rages stifled,

twisted & singed shut? I had thought

it was a woman's voice—
though I had hoped

all my life that my father would feed me
the milk my mother could not

make from her body.
Once, when I opened the door & saw

him shaving, naked, the sole of his foot
resting on the toilet, I thought

those things hanging down were
udders. From then on I understood there was a

female part he hid—something
soft & unprotected

I shouldn't see.

Sunday afternoons at Claire Carlyle's

My mother & father, light-
skinned, but too new

to make the upper cut,

were, nevertheless, welcomed
into the marble foyer

under an icebox-sized chandelier
to mix martinis with double-edged

men and women trained to outwit
and out-white the whites. Almost all

were light & straight-featured
enough to pass—some did,

some didn't.
Claire's brother Bob

passed. If seen weekdays,
he wasn't

to be spoken to. Light and dark
did the same—an inward

move to protect those
fortunate enough to choose.

But why did my mother

(who looked as white
as Loretta Young—& as beautiful) see

Bob one weekday walking
toward her up Woodward

and cross
to the other side? Why,

when anyone would
only have seen

two white people?
It was something in my mother

not visible: in her

mind's eye
she was black & wore the robe

of it over her fine features. Perhaps,
she crossed in case

some inner misstep

might betray him
(the inner world

being vast & treacherous)—

as if they were slaves running
for their lives.

For my unnamed brother (1943–1943)

i was left out
i was chosen second & then left out
i was left
handed i was left
to fend for myself i
was the second in
command the second
in line i came
without direction
      *
i want the
milk i want my
first pick i want
choice & all its implications there was a
      *
residue of
scar
between us it chafed
when we rubbed our
chests together
      *
                      hello, brother, hello?
hello in there, brother, can you
hear me? it's a long
tunnel to the grave   speak

you were my
first god i was rapt in your
coming
            (mother better
eat her vegetables, she better chew) choo
choo

what's bitter between us

                    *
                                    i want the

milk i need it for my
teeth they're
soft the gums
bleed there's the evidence

on my toothbrush i got the
second draft i need calcium
to make up i

got a job
        & left
i don't know where you're
buried
            *
what do you
need? what will make you
happy? what do you
want? the dead
do have mouths &
appetites suck it
up there's plenty in the ice
box more
where that came from
            *
                        if somebody
asked me what's
next i wouldn't
know i took my hands off
her like something
hot or fragile or in
pain i was

aghast at suffering how you can feed
& feed it
      & it's never
full
    *

       there's a separation
between us a suppuration there's just the
space of an idea i don't know what's
missing it's a blind
spot sometimes my left eye
focuses & it's like looking at
both of us through a
window
    *

         i'm telling you the
facts of life for
you haven't been told
you're in your late
fifties you're dis-
eased or disinterested a
queer unable to
come out of the casket OK
    *

you live this
life i'll live the
next she only has enough milk for
one baby i'll go
around this
time you come the
next that time you'll have a
better mother i

promise you that

28

Dolls

To be born woman is to know—
Although they do not speak of it at school—
Women must labor to be beautiful.
—W. B. Yeats

Teng ai, *a love imbedded in preverbal knowledge,*
accompanied by unspeakable pain, and shared
only through the empathy between the two bodies
(mother and daughter) alike.
—Wang Ping

I.

Take care of your little mother, my aunt told me
shortly before she died. My little five-foot-four-inch mother,
whose clothes I outgrew when I was ten, already
proud of my big bones—(Nothing could overpower
me if I was made of my father's bones). My mother was astounded—
I should put bricks on your head & she kept dressing me
in pinafores & ruffled socks. *Toi,* she called me,
as if I was supposed to stay small.

II.

Sometimes it seemed I couldn't have come out of
her, that something was wrong. When I stood behind her I felt
ungainly, like something that flopped about without
gravity. I was excessive, too much.
I thieved her clothes until it was impossible to make them
fit—hers was the only body I knew how to make beautiful.

III.

My grandmother bought me a doll I couldn't touch. She
had peaches & cream skin, breasts, a taffeta dress,
& porcelain green eyes. Her fingers were delicate & curved
like eyebrows. I broke my dolls, so we had to put her up
high to admire, like a storeowner sticks a manikin
on a black pole to show off what he's got.

IV.

My mother gave me dolls that peed, that you had to feed,
that you had to bathe in a little plastic Bathinette.
Everything smelled clean like rubber. You had to
learn to be a mother. Even the pee. One of the bottles
refilled itself when you turned it upright. It was o.k. for a
doll to pee. The more work you did the better mother you were.

V.

I was hard on my dolls. The ones that had stuffed bodies
came up missing arms. Monkey-bear had his insides ripped out.
Big Rabbit couldn't stand. His legs & feet were
bent forward so that, when we played school—with his
Little Buddha smile that,
no matter how much I swung him around in a circle & beat him
against the floor, just stayed there—he would topple off his
seat & have to be shaken again.

VI.

The dolls that cried *mamma* came up with a busted rattle in
their throat, their eyes clunked open so that they couldn't go to
sleep but stared perpetually up at the ceiling like middle-aged
insomniacs. One doll had a problem with her eyes, they were out
of kilter, so that they didn't open unless you whacked
her on the back. Then they were stuck open, so she seemed
dead. We had to work on her too hard to make her do the most
ordinary things—just to open her eyes! Her eyes clunked shut &,
way back in the pit of her skull, we could hear her thinking.

VII.

When I was born my mother sat up, hysterical, on the delivery
table. She said it was the drugs. She couldn't stop laughing.
Her toxemic body had been pumped out & I was a robin's egg
blue, a pale, delicate thing whose blood vessels you
could see from the outside. My "inner life" stared up at you
through translucent skin, the way you can see a face
floating up to a lake's surface.

                    I put my inner life right in her hands.

VIII.

No, that isn't the way my father saw it. He said
when he looked in the nursery he saw a baby so hairy
he thought it should be swinging from a chandelier.
Though he really loved me for my excesses—
for eating too much, for stealing French fries from his plate
(*That girl can really hold her liquor,* he'd brag
when I was twelve. *They call her old hollow leg),*
& even my hair—he'd lift me up by it
& carry me up four flights of stairs. He loved my hair.

IX.

My mother suffered, oh did she suffer, the way all
light-skinned women were supposed to suffer. She suffered that
& more. She proved that she didn't like it. She proved that of all
the un-black women, the ones babies didn't just come
popping out of—

    & even of the ones that babies came roaring
through like a train, of even them—she was one of the most,
most suffering.

X.

During pregnancy, she wore the right shoes. She ate the
right foods. She read the book that the doctor gave her with
pictures of white women in plain suits. She tucked it in a place
sacred & hidden, in her sewing box. She pierced it with needles
& thread either punishing it or marking it
with a hundred little, colored banners.

                                        She used to like sex, my
father once said, puzzled.

XI.

My mother with the peaches & cream skin, my mother with
the eyebrows of a blackbird's wing, my mother with eyelashes
that brushed halfway down her cheeks, my mother with the high,
creamy breasts, my mother in her slip & socks on her knees
scrubbing the kitchen floor, or weeping in the doorway,

my lovely, delicate, little mother.

Mistrust of the beloved

I must explain to you what I must explain to myself: that there, where love, desire and want spring from the most natural source, there, in that spot, in that moment, is the scalding fire; and, instead, springs to life the unwanted and beaten girl, her whole soul face and body shiny with burn scar, inflexible, taut and hard, immersed anew in the conflagration; for, as long as the route turns to that inward burning, it cannot take her out again into that place where her father proved he did not love.

The heart of one so riddled must keep to itself: We spoil what we want for the deeper motive, for it is deep in the brain where instinct lives, as another withdraws a hand from fire.

PART II

A Memory of the Future

Your mind failed, not your muscle!

—Hiroshi Fotogoishi

I see my father after his death

I caught a plane at about eleven in the morning, and we were at the
funeral home at about two. My father had been dead about ten hours.
We had chosen the mortician who had been my grandfather's old
competitor, whose son, unlike my father, had stayed in the family
business. I wanted to see my father before he was "ready," but the
mortician didn't want to take me back. He talked about germs, about
me washing my hands after. I didn't know if he was afraid of my
emotions—that I would burst into uncontrollable tears?—or if there
was something back there he didn't want me to see. Maybe it was
dirty, or maybe it just wasn't the rule—so often people can't break the
rules.

It was clean, like an old-fashioned kitchen, with tile and stainless
steel sinks and counters. There was a huge blue bottle in the corner
with a siphon in it, a black-and-white tile floor. It looked efficient, not
spiffed up like his French provincial waiting room. Then I came upon
my father, swaddled in a layer of linen, zipped in plastic and bound
with tape, his face the only part of him free.

The color was pure, as if he had been drained of age and illness. That
look of dark acceptance, that fixed stare that penetrated without hope
or understanding, had been left behind. There was a softness I had
never seen, his forehead, unlined and smooth. He had been given a
second beauty as a death-gift. The monster had flown out on its hard
dark wings, and left behind, not a shell, but one tortured a lifetime and
released.

*

Even when he had been in a coma—his legs inflexible, locked in fetal
position, nurses turning his body every few hours like something
basted over coals—I would take the covers back and look at him. It
was under the pretext of seeing if he had bedsores, or if he was losing
weight but, really, all I wanted to do was fix my eyes on his body—the

same big toe as mine, the same twisted little toe, his thick knees, each like the end of a club. I stared as long as I wanted, unashamed, unafraid of my great love, unafraid he would leave me.

My father had lost his sexual beauty in his sixties. But in the days of his illness his body became lustrous, so full of energy and brightness that it seemed too hot to put my hands on.

After his surgery he had said, "You're not going to like what you see," but when he lifted his shirt I kissed the long, raw cut, which looked like two slabs of butchered ribs stapled together, and said, "You're still beautiful to me." I had always loved what he could never love in himself—even his wounds.

*

Though he had been dead for ten hours, someone told me it takes thirteen for the spirit to move on. So he had not gone yet; he was still partly there, seeping out in shallow expirations.

Certainly what one sees later, after the embalming, is an object made by the undertaker; it has nothing to do with the one dead. Though I hadn't been with him at death, I was there to see him before the embalming and, for the rest of my life, to know that look of calm that had come.

My cruel father had looked forward, seen heaven, and sent back this sign of peace.

*

That night I had a dream, but not a dream, for it was as real as this very moment, with all my feelings in it; and I didn't have any idea of how or why or when. Suddenly, as if I had just been born and didn't know anything before that, I didn't feel fear. Nothing else had happened, just that fear had been sucked out of me, and I didn't even remember

44

it happening but just felt gratitude for an absence that made my life—I swear I am not making a metaphor—feel like heaven.

But as the night went on—it didn't feel like night, it felt like a trueness that made everything different and new—a worry began to encroach, a sliver of gray: "What if this fearlessness were taken away?" When I woke I felt such joy; I shook my husband and said, "I'm free, I'm different." And then I began to put my feet over the side of the bed, slowly, the ground coming up to meet me and, at that moment, when my feet touched the floor, something in me said, "Your father is dead," and I knew why I had felt so happy.

*

I had forgotten that moment until today, that happiness that had tarnished like silver, like an old old mirror in which I could no longer see my face. I don't know why I lost it, why that heaviness came back— for wasn't my father truly dead, didn't I no longer have to fear him?— but, in a few days, the wonder faded. My mind was not ready for such light. I had to dig my way out of darkness one weighty grain at a time, as if a memory of the future had visited.

My dad & sardines

my dad's going to give me a self
back.
i've made an altar called
The Altar for Healing the Father & Child,
& asked him what i could do
for him so he would
do nice for me. he said i should stop
saying bad things about him &, since
i've said just about everything bad
i can think of &, since . . . well,
no, i change my
mind, i can't promise
him that. but even healing is
negotiable, so, if he's in
heaven (or trying
to get in), it wouldn't hurt
to be in touch. the first thing i want is to be able to
enjoy the little things again—for example, to stop peeling
down the list of things i
have to do &
enjoy this poem, enjoy how, last night, scouring
the cupboards, i found a
can of sardines that
must be five
years old &, since i was home after a long
trip &, since it was 1 a.m. & i hadn't eaten
dinner &, since there was no other
protein in the house,
i cranked it open & remembered that
my dad loved
sardines—right before bed—with
onions & mustard. i can't get into
my dad's old heart, but i remember that look

on his face when he would
load mustard on a saltine cracker, lay a little
fish on top, & tip it with a juicy slice
of onion. then he'd look up from his soiled
fingers with one eyebrow
raised, a rakish
grin that said—*all*
for me!—as if he was
getting away
with murder.

On a picture of the Buddhist monk Pema Chödrön

do I want to look like this? women
with that playfulness in their faces not
childish but elfin as if they have learned
how to shift the world slightly & let it
slip down the ice of its own melting women
who have been lost but not
hidden clear-skinned
wide-awake their unmade selves
neither genderless nor fixed i don't know where
their genitals are if heart
is the center do they feel the tug
of longing there? what blossoms?
where?
from the brain?
belly button?
is the clitoris throbbing?

On the revolution of the Jersey cows

Half a mile past the road to Still Point,
I run into the Jersey cows,
robed in black & white like Old Dominicans.
With muddy boots
in clops of hoof-torn grass,
they eye me as I pass,
their sensitive ears turning
like fine-tuned telescopes.
"Hi, cow," I call to one, respectfully,
for I think she likes that,
& she turns her head to me,
the thick muscles of her neck & shoulders
pulling like a heavy rug.
A few feet farther, twenty
with their heads stuck through clanking metal pipes
churn soft, flexible mouths, bony jaws—
& in their eyes that dimness
like a sprig of faint black stars.
Are they waiting for a leader,
or just to be steered up the thick-pounded slope
into the barn?
The one I spoke to has forgotten me.
She drops her nose into a muddy runnel
& laps from the cold, familiar, spicy pool.

The new pet

i don't want to worry about a fish yet
here i am when i am tired going down & up two
flights of stairs to bring him clean spring water
to fill up his bowl maybe he looked un-
happy because there was no current—the water was not
high enough to reach the motor—& he has grown used to
the big tank, the heater & water filter, for he began to flip
about & even leap up to my finger when he was hungry.
surely nothing will come to me for doing
good to a fish, & still i do it; though i often wish i had
a mean heart

The Telly Cycle

Joy is an act of resistance.

Why would a black woman
need a fish
to love? Why did she need a

flash of red, living, in the
corner of her eye? As if she could love nothing
up close, but had to step

away from it, come
back to drop a few seeds
& let it grab

on to her, as if it caught
her
on some hook that couldn't

hurt. Why did she need a fish,
a red
thorn or, among the thorns, that

flower? What does her love have to do
with five hundred years of
sorrow, then joy coming up like a

small breath, a
bubble? What does it have to do
with the graveyards of the

Atlantic in her mother's
heart?

For Telly the fish

Telly's favorite artist was Alice Neel.
When he first came to my house,
I propped up her bright yellow shade with open
window & a vase of flowers (postcard size)
behind his first fish bowl. I thought
it might give him something
to look at, like the center
of a house you keep coming
back to, a hearth, a root
for your eye. It was a
wondering in me that came up with that
thought, a kind of empathy
across my air & through his
water, maybe the first
word I cast out between us
in case he could
hear. Telly would stare at that painting
for hours, hanging there with his glassy
eyes wide
open. At night he wanted the
bottom, as if it were a warm
bed, he'd lay there
sort of dreaming, his eyes
gray & dim &
thoughtless. For months he came back
to her, the way a critic or lover
can build a whole
lifetime on the study of one
great work. I don't know why
he stopped, maybe it was when
he first noticed
me, the face above my hand
feeding for, sometimes, when I'd set the food

on top, he'd still watch me, eye
to eye, as if saying, food
isn't enough. Once, when I
bent, he jumped up out of the water & kissed
my lips. What is a fish's kiss like?
You'd think it would be
cold, slimy, but it was
quick, nippy, hard. Maybe it was just
what I expected. For all
our fears of
touch, it takes so long
to learn how to take in.

When he stopped coming
to the top, I guess I did all the wrong
things—the fish medicine
that smelled, measured
carefully for his ounce of weight—
for his gills worked
so hard & he lay still,
tipped over slightly
like a dead boat.
How do you stop the hurt
of having to breathe?

After, I took him to the middle of the
yellow bridge right near the
Andy Warhol museum—
I had put a paper towel
in a painted egg & laid him in it—
&, at the top,
I opened the casket & emptied him out
into the water.

Special ears

I liked him for his tailfin, which was long like a mermaid's & flowed like a
silver blue ruffle in the water,
larger than you'd expect a little fish's tail to be—

    generous, excessive, a bit astonishing, like a girl with too much hair!

Sometimes he would rise like a submarine, straight up, as if he would nip
my finger, *get out of my water,* his mouth would open like a little scoop of
blackness & let out one bubble, like a smoke ring of my father's, a message
from the underworld.

Another poem of a small grieving for my fish Telly

Perhaps I should forgive
Telly for dying in my care, *Just a*
fish, someone said, *Just*

get another. Lucille said
our power becomes
greater when we lose the flesh; so,

when I poured Telly out
of his painted casket (a little wooden
egg) out over the rail

into the all
becoming, was it a miracle
that he had lived, was it a miracle?

Once, when I prayed for a sign,

God opened the closed
vault of the sky, the sun popped out
& shone directly in my face, & hail, yes,

hail started falling (in July). I was
afraid to believe in love. *God,*
don't waste your miracles on me. &

the sun went back, like a face
retreating. Telly, you are bodi-
less, you are with my mother

& father. Say it wasn't my
fault you suffered, with your little
working gills, say you forgive me.

On the reasons I loved Telly the fish

Why would I say I was
"pathetic," when talking about my
life, why would I think of it as
"little"—my "little life," I said,
as if, looking back
at what kept me alive,
what I constructed to make my own
success, to regard that with
tenderness &
understanding—as something even
sweet &
marvelous—was
insane? Then maybe I began to
love Telly—
really nothing in the
grand scheme of things—the way that lady, when I told her that
I paid 100 dollars a month for someone to come in &
feed Telly when I was away, said—"but, Toi, how much
did Telly cost? $1.98? Well then why not just
flush him every time & get another?"
Whatever I said
to myself, whatever
I felt & did, that
kind of care was
silly,
nice, but, well, you know,
crazy, the way, when you grow up &
understand the great
things, a fish's life is
nothing, as if (& probably they can't
think or feel) there are much more
important things to

do to think about to
love & dedicate ourselves
to: there are
doctors, great
poets, there is
fine furniture, true love, children,
god, for
god's sake, there is everything to
remember, everything to be
worried & concerned about, as if I could
find it if I just kept
looking, something really
real out there always just outside of what I could
take in. & this was how I
stayed alive.

My aunt took me to
her job from the time I was about
three. I'd go down to the
basement where she was
head of the mail department—first black woman to have such an
executive job in Detroit, even though it was
in the basement—I'd take up a little
desk in the corner & do whatever she said, open
the flaps of envelopes by the box—five hundred in a box, maybe
twenty boxes a day for ten cents a box &, with each box, I'd
compete with myself, each day,
to make more
money, & make enough
to buy my own
lunch, a corned beef sandwich at the
Broadway Market with

two halves of a new
dill & a fruit
punch, & sit there at the
marble counter enjoying
the warmth of meat,
the slop of mustard,
& the way the
rind of the bread was
just a little tough to
tear with your teeth.
I worked without
word,
away from the grownups, able to
make my own
way & feel
competent, as if I had a
place & something I could truly
do without making somebody
mad or un-
happy. &, just looking
back on myself, as if I were an eye
looking from a high
place, seeing that little
girl, counting the envelopes, boxes, making her
fingers go faster,
counting the boxes over & over because she'd
forget & had to make certain,
enjoying how many boxes were piling
up, how, yesterday, she did a box in ten minutes &
today she could do more than
two boxes in twenty (there was always a way to

try harder & give the day a good
reason.)

When I looked back
on that little five-year-old, six, seven, eight, nine,
it was as if I were a little
busy fish being watched by an
interested & even caring
owner. I had finally
bought myself.

Because I was good to Telly in his life,

because I taught him Alice Neel
& fed him frozen mealworms,
(until I found out he'd
lose his bright red tail color
for that pleasure),
because I never left him
alone when I traveled (never liking those
who said their betta did just fine
sitting on the edge of their office desk
over the long weekend—how would *you*
like it not to eat for three
days, I wanted to ask), for choosing
carefully among the pet
sitters, interviewing, looking for one who took a fish
seriously
& told betta stories about how smart they
are, coming up
to say hi in the morning, checking you
out with a certain calm or anxious
look in the eye, because
I believed
in one fish's
brain & life & skills &
emptied him out into the
thawing river saying
prayers for my
lover or husband or brother
of a year,
because of this I am certain
he sent me a
gift from the china blue
rivers of heaven, a lovely man, who
first kissed me on

that bridge,
sending a photo
after rain of "Kissing
Bridge underwater" scrawled with his loose
sprawling letters; because all things are
connected, a
circle,
bread on the water, as my mother said,
always comes home.

An apology to Telly the revolutionary

Love or respect, my father said,
you can't have both.

Last night, after the reading,

the audience
climbed to their feet

& cheered you—as if
you were a rock star!

Viva Telly!
Telly lives!

One woman explained,
you only let them *think* you were

a fish; but, right now,
you are in

Jamaica or Cuba with
Assata Shakur.

They giggled
at our kiss & I thought:

now they see the *real*
me, not a poet, just

some pathetic old woman
who made a lover

of a fish. So I reasoned. After all,
you weren't real, you were only

a symbol.

Telly,

I never meant
to betray you. Just

to distract them
as I handed myself

a robe.

When the goddess makes love to me,

she has to pass through my father,
she has to find him
where he sits in a corner inside me
cold as a turd.
I can't reach him anymore.
I don't have the strength to yank him out
& blow on his breasts.
She has to tuck her fingers between his thighs
& warm him, slowly—
first the shoulders & the tops of his arms.
She has to coax the crying boy
to come through the dead
walking on tiptoe.
Sometimes he can't find his way
feeling in the dark with his blunt
fingers,
& sometimes he stands there, dumb-
struck, his body trembling between
us like a little bird's.

Untitled

Ten days after her death, i nap on my mother's
bed & for the first time it seems in years in
front of the gentle eyes of the Blessed Virgin (my mother's
Palm Sunday palms folded behind the frame) i feel my
clitoris throb *aroused? in my mother's bed?*
before the Virgin?
i press my thighs together as if my hands must
remain clean i touch the tip of my
left breast until the nipple grows hard & lifts
my thighs tighten embraced
in this pleasure
as in a prayer that goes up from my whole body
i have gone beyond some dirtiness
some act i cannot conceive my mother would have
condoned yet here now
i have touched some deeper female presence
that her death gives me as a gift

The night I stopped singing like Billie Holiday

*Coming to one's voice is . . . not a linear process,
not a matter of learning skills, forms, and laws
of grammar and syntax. It is a dynamic process
in which much of what is occurring and has
occurred remains invisible.*
—*The Black Notebooks*

I was playing a CD and enjoying her voice, taking Richard home and
talking about the difference between Billie Holiday early and late, and
I was thinking about which songs of hers I could learn and sing when
I read with the drum player in DC. Just before Richard got out, I said,
"You never heard me sing like Billie Holiday, did you?" "No," he said,
"but Ben Shannon said that on the first night of class, you closed your
eyes and sung a cappella, and that there had never been anything like
it."

Alone, driving home with the roof of the car open, feeling that
wonderful softness and openness of the summer night, I was deciding
whether I should turn down my street and into the gated parking lot
or just turn up Billie and keep driving, driving over one or two of the
beautiful yellow bridges of Pittsburgh, so architecturally perfect—
like the large-scale bridges of New York, the Brooklyn and GW, but
small-scale, doable, all of them nearly empty on a summer night, so
that you could have the bridge all to yourself. Imagine a bridge all
yours on such a night, like a beautiful woman. During the movie, for
some reason, I had put my hands under my arms, and I had felt my
own body, that beautiful, fat curve under a woman's arm that is also
an extended part of the breast, the soft, full crease, and I liked feeling
that in myself, as I might like feeling it in another woman, and when I
pulled my hand out I could smell myself on it. I was beginning again to
have an odor, the juices, the sexual juices, were starting to come back,
so that, once again, I would attract or repel like some flower.

Then, right before I turned into my driveway, a terrible premonition
came that, if I opened my mouth and started singing, I wouldn't sound
like Billie Holiday.

For years that sound had exuded out of me, as if she were in there just waiting for me to open my mouth. Always there was the strain. Some part of me clamped down on top of what was coming up, and it seemed that is what made Billie happen—I thought even Billie had had that slight squeeze—but something had changed and, when I started to sing, I didn't sound like her.

*

I don't remember ever hearing *me* sing—I think it must have been me singing—characterless. I sounded like any person with an OK voice, but nothing special. Before, even if I wasn't as good as Billie, at least I sounded like her, and there was such an aching try—like the pain that made her turn a note into something sweet, short, and unforgettable— that people could feel it. They had been mesmerized. They said maybe I should stop writing poetry and go on the road as a Billie Holiday impersonator. Now my phrasing was off, like somebody trying to win a Billie Holiday contest; the twin-ness had broken, and I sounded like her stranger. My body had forgotten what was most natural for it to do, as if the only way I could be Billie was by not being me.

*

There is a story I heard from a South American Indian that, when someone dies, you have to cry for a year; your tears are the boat that carries that person across the waters, and, after a year, when they reach the other side, they are not the person you loved anymore, they are your ancestor.

Every crossing is like that, the great loss of leaving one shore and heading out to nowhere. It is a frightening thing to give up something, even if it is an imitation—especially if you are famous for it. But what if I don't have a real thing, you think to yourself. And, at that moment, all you know is that you have nothing, that you have lost the only thing you had.

*

Everyone in my family said I couldn't sing. From the time I was a
baby. "She can't carry a tune in a bucket." "Sing solo, so low we can't
hear you." Though the teasing hurt and made me unsure of myself, it
also made me feel loved, connected, and special. Maybe I sensed that
they needed someone to look down on, that the teasing had done them
good. Besides, my voice was so small; it didn't weigh anything against
their sureties. My voice would squeak out; but, already, I didn't believe
anything I said. I fought them good-naturedly, trying to sing to defend
myself, but, usually, I ended up giving them the pleasure of covering
up their ears and howling, "No, no, no more, please." Being an object of
their teasing was a way of hoping something worse wouldn't happen.

*

This past week, I went to a concert by Sweet Honey in the Rock. The
next day a friend called and said Ysaye Barnwell wants to meet you.
She says she's quoting *The Black Notebooks* in a piece she's writing,
and she wants to talk to you about it.

I went down to the bookstore where she was signing her book, *No
Mirrors in My Nana's House*, and she put her arms around me in a big
sister hug. "I'm going to quote that part where you say the development
of the voice is not linear. I was writing about this very thing in the
voices of singers. We're saying exactly the same thing."

It strikes me as wonderful and terrifying—and obvious—that the voice
of the poet is very much connected to the voice of the singer; perhaps,
in the most basic way, voice equals voice.

And suddenly I see my voice inside my chest, it's a little child, perhaps
the age of a toddler, I don't know if it's a boy or girl, but it's hiding
under a rock. Ysaye said that the voice is meant to fill all of space. It's
a powerful thing to fill up all of the space outside us with our voices,

but, first, we have to be able to fill the space inside. And yet isn't hiding a useful thing? Don't we hide what we are afraid to lose or have taken away? And when it's time, perhaps we see the thing hidden, and then we make a choice about what to do with it.

*

I began to listen to Billie Holiday when I was fourteen. I listened for hours every day. I learned every song, nuance, turn, I sang with the records. I sang with her for twenty years; she was always with me. I loved her, though I didn't understand her life, and though I learned things that confused me: that when she spoke, she spoke in a harsh, coarse manner, cursing, with a bitter tongue, her words flat, broad-stroked; that eloquent voice that came when she started singing was from another universe in her throat.

It reminded me of a story about a dentist my husband used to go to. He had palsy, and when his patients saw him coming toward their mouths with the looming buzz saw in his trembling hand, they were ready to jump out of their seats. However, as soon as he set the instrument on the ridge of one tooth, his hand became perfectly steady. Now I think, for Billie, one voice didn't have anything to do with the other, or perhaps one voice had to be the opposite of the other, or perhaps they were controlled by different brains: the genius brain that put a billion bits of information in the turn of a grace note was not the same brain that said, "Put the god damn glass down mother fucker." From where did that one brain drink? What did it have access to? Did the one brain know about the other?

*

My friend, Susan Wind, brings me a present before I leave town. I had told her about my voice being like a child, hiding under a rock in my chest, and she hands me, gift-wrapped, a palm-sized, iridescent rock with streaming colors in it—as if it has a hurricane inside—taped to the top of a cassette of lullabies. Music to comfort the child and a rock that holds the power of wind and water: now I am both under it and holding it in my hand.

*

Days later, I decide to do a reading for no other reason but joy, no other reason than to have fun. My mother, son, and grandson are in the audience, and I decide to open with my favorite Billie Holiday song. I say, "This is a reading dedicated to love, love exquisite and love hard, and I'm going to begin by singing Billie Holiday's 'Deep Song.'"

Lonely grief is hounding me,
Like a lonely shadow hounding me...

I realized something I had forgotten, that meaning is not in the words, but in the sounds; that if we just sing the sounds we put in, the listener will get all the complexity. For that is how we wrote the words, with our hearts singing, and we must not flatten out meaning, must not destroy or deaden, we must let out all the sounds, so that what we said and meant with our whole body can be heard. And in that spirit I sung my reading and, after, I received a standing ovation; never have I received applause like that. No one told me, "You sound like Billie Holiday," but many said, "You have a beautiful voice." My mother said that when I had said I was going to sing, she almost stood up and said, "No, please don't"—she was very afraid she was going to be embarrassed—but when I opened my mouth, she couldn't believe it. She thought I must have had voice lessons.

*

It wasn't like Billie's—though it did sound as if I was squeezing up something in me, and that did sound a bit like her—the way she asked men to beat her up before she went on stage so that she would remember the pain—but mine was more open at the throat, so that something came up that was me, and Billie didn't interfere.

70

When I touched her

When I touched her for the first
time I swooned with
wonder, for the full lips swelled, a dark
fruit bloomed under my
fingers. I could not
breathe with my hand there.
She let me stroke the
lips inside the
lips, that double swelling beneath the
clitoris like the violin's under-
tone, which lifts the whole body from its
anal seat. She
moaned without thought
& spoke to guide me higher, so that my fingers could
find the hill whereon the goddess looked out
with equanimity & calm.

The iris and chicken fat

I.

Suddenly I see that each see-through petal has a line of gold fur going
down its middle, like the fine fur that appears between the pubic hair
and the belly button of a woman who has given birth—a dead giveaway,
for it never disappears;

and, between the cup itself and its stem, there is a veined gray-green
sheath, nearly transparent, shriveling, still glistening inside, as if it
had held, besides the black embryo, a cooling light.

II.

And I remember how my mother, once, after a particularly violent
screaming argument about whether or not the chicken fat should be
cut away before the chicken is roasted, said, or proposed, really, "Why
don't we just drop our anger and go out and enjoy the day?"

And I remember how, when anger lifts, there is that gap, a space so
clear that it seems the air itself is pushed back and, in its place, there
is the lightest weight of knowing.

Lighting the tulips

It's all about longing, how, just before it enters the brain, shot straight out of the heart, it falls into sparks, maybe just behind the vocal cords where it touches the new words and transmutes into feeling: four shining branches that break and splinter like ice. I meditate and, after memory fades, there are these four sparklers firing.

This is being with the self—as your hands would cup spring flowers.

I slip the dark pink tulips from their sleeve, set them cautiously on the rim of the sink, bring the right-sized glass vase and, carefully, lift each one; really tenderly. I think of their soft-spined stems, of just how much force the fingers must close with, how much tension in the muscles between the power of dropping and lifting that will bring forth, moment by moment, a slow awareness of this certain caring, of the scissors on a stem, of the amazing lightness of this one's being between my fingers.

Gershwin

It's a good thing to be friends with the dead. I'm starting to realize
that, with friends, being dead isn't that important. Take me and
Gershwin, for example, who died at thirty-eight from a brain
tumor (the popular story: he keeled over at a cocktail party playing
"Rhapsody in Blue"). And isn't that the best way to go—the notes so
alive in your hands that fear is blown right out of the socket?

It's either a very small or a very large place we live in—our cosmos,
our kitchen—so many generations packed up close. You realize lots of
things as you get ready. The creaky doors of the heart open—just like a
one-track mind. *I'm nobody, and yet I have this particular place on this
particular bench and nobody can do it better.*

I'm listening to that last, hopeful song of Porgy's, the cripple in rags
taking off in his rickety goat cart; fearless—no matter how far—he's
going to find his love.

Oh Lawd, I'm on my way,
I'm on my way,
To a heavenly land . . .

How wonderful that either you understood this age so well that you
captured the vibrations, or else you invented what we know. Did some
lingering ancestor flood your heart with a blue note? Did some black
woman play the scale for you?

I wonder if it's so convincing, with its sad happiness—as if there's a
town right to the side of the stage where we'll be able to drop Porgy a
line—because Gershwin is telling us how happy he is to be driving his
own poor cart. *Oh Lawd, I'm on my way . . .* Only thirty-eight, his work
here over.

A little prayer to Our Lady

so all day i
go by the
xmas tree bulb (orange) in the
little altar of
shells
that i set up &
keep lit at the
top of the stairs, so that rising now i
rise
to praise
her, to
remember the sacredness of my
work.
perhaps she likes orange light
thrown softly against her for
she looks divine.
my house seems richer
more alive
less lonely
with her here
i am allowed
to believe.

To a cruel lover

What girl wouldn't want to get
a letter from the lover
who had humiliated her
forty years ago? *I guess you're not speaking
to us colored folks anymore,* he had said,
strolling right past me & the white friend
I was walking with.
What girl wouldn't want
to get a letter that said, *I read about a famous
Toi Derricotte in the news & wonder if that
is the same Toi* **Webster** *who lived
on Taylor, who was my friend.*   It's sad
how the longing for someone as cruel
kept coming, as if,
when I swallowed that dead cat, my heart,
the cruelness would go away,
like a prizefighter who holds the devil
close to his chest, a hug
so that he can't strike.
It's a sad weapon.
Two years after I found someone
just as bad as you.
Who knows
whether evil was in your
heart, & if it was, why
it was put there, maybe
by someone more cruel
than you were to me.
Probably to this day
you don't know your wrong,
like my mother & father,
you remember
only the good. I loved to dance

&, once, giving you another chance,
when you walked toward me
on a dance floor,
I stood there,
hopeful, my arms
opening to take you in.
You glided right
past me to another girl. Humiliation
was your middle name.
Now you write
hoping I've forgotten, or that I've not
forgotten. No,
I am not the same.

Cherry blossoms

I went down to
mingle my breath
with the breath
of the cherry blossoms.

There were photographers:
Mothers arranging their
children against
gnarled old trees;
a couple, hugging,
asks a passerby
to snap them
like that,
so that their love
will always be caught
between two friendships:
ours & the friendship
of the cherry trees.

Oh Cherry,
why can't my poems
be as beautiful?

A young woman in a fur-trimmed
coat sets a card table
with linens, candles,
a picnic basket & wine.
A father tips
a boy's wheelchair back
so he can gaze
up at a branched
heaven.
          All around us

the blossoms
flurry down
whispering,

  Be patient,
you have an ancient beauty.

     Be patient,
    you have an ancient beauty.

**How Craig Foster enabled me to write the poems I'm writing now
& gave me this voice**

When I told him I bought a
betta, he
sent all kinds of emails about its
beauty & natural traits: how it's a killer
& has to room
alone, about that beautiful big blue or red
floaty tail, bigger than its body; how the male—believe it or not—blows
bubbles for the eggs to rest in, making a clear
quilt over the top
just in case some nice
female comes along. He sent news
that, to me, read like
poetry: how they can stay
in tiny fishbowls because, in Thailand & Cambodia, they live
in puddles in the rice paddies &,
when their puddle gets dirty, they just hop
into the next. It
made me see Telly
in a new light &, given
sight, I began
to think a language for part of myself
that, before, could not
speak.

I have never been able to write
about his mother's
death.
She was my best friend since grade school; then, in her thirties,
hooked up with the wrong
man & got
murdered. Craig grew up without a
mother & died
of diabetes in his early forties.

Once, in our twenties, when I was crying about a
man who had left me, she commanded me
to stop. She was a strong
black woman & didn't believe
in tears.

Twenty years after she died, a woman came up to me
after a reading &
asked me to sign a book.
She pronounced her name
several times:
"Amonda, not Amanda"—just the way

my friend said hers. Then she said, "Write:
'Because you taught me
how to cry.'"

Had I lived
& she died
because of that one difference
between us?

PART III

The Undertaking

*But to say what you want to say you must
create another language and nourish it for
years and years with what you have loved,
with what you have lost, with what you will
never find again.*

—George Seferis, *Days of 1945–1951*

The exigencies of form

It is not the corpse, it is not the artifact, it is the soft thing with feathers. It is hope, it is what is said at the tenderest point; it is covered up with language and syntax, it is metered and measured, it has on its finest dress; it may look like a king going out on a fine horse, or a diplomat in a car with black windows; it may cover itself and hide, but it is reaching, it is alive.

The undertaking

My brother Jay, my half-brother, eighteen years younger than I am, brings our father's ashes when he visits me in Pittsburgh. They have been on a shelf in his basement for twenty years, wrapped in the kind of plain brown wrapper universally understood to be hiding something "dirty." We slash open the paper to uncover a drawer-shaped plastic box. Jay pulls a string and the top pops off as easily as the lid on a box of oatmeal and reveals, too quickly, the chalky issue, the pebbles of our father.

We have walked to the neighborhood golf course—my father loved golf more than anything good for him—and decide to drop him off at the top of a little bridge over a spout of clear water. Jay pours most of the ash, I run down to dislodge the fallen plastic bag from a few prickly weeds and shake out a half-cup more. We hold each other around the waist and Jay says his prayer of the moment, "Rest here now safe near your daughter. Whatever you did, whatever you have done, God chose you to be our father for a good reason. We love you and will never forget you." I feel a vacancy, a quiet that may signal an end. I court nothing, no drama, and yet I wait to see if it's over, really over.

*

Many abused children never love again, never trust. Their hands pass it down to their children. The body holds memories; it will never be caught again. Talk isn't enough. You can never comprehend. At some point something happens: a door closes, your boyfriend goes out for a smoke, and, in less than a second, your stomach tightens like a grill. Alarm bells ring in the amygdala: Daddy's home.

*

Is it possible to change everything that has happened by looking at the past in a different way? Not denying anything but, perhaps, inserting some detail that pries open the heart so that more light floods out of it?

*

How do you end a book? How do you end a lifelong obsession? Writing itself is a triumph; it changes the past by changing the act of repression. It cries out against violence. It confronts the command to subjugate oneself. When you have been silent, dead for so long, encased and buried, the oppressor's voice is the first one you hear. It is the way you speak to yourself. Then the most childish voice arises. It has to start from the same place it was buried.

*

I took my first poetry workshop when I was twenty-seven. The first time I heard "Daddy" by Sylvia Plath, I was shocked and profoundly awakened. I didn't know there was any place, any way for such fury to be expressed, and I had no idea that such an expression could be made into something that had order and beauty, where the broken pieces could make sense. The poem could not only hold an unspeakable truth, it could also bring forth the very voice that had been put down, it could bring it to life.

*

You don't just write a book, you live it. I know a book is finished when I've changed. The obsession lifts, it lets me go, a door to the outside world opens. Only the creation of a work of art can spring the trap; only the girl locked inside knows when the door slams open, when the power is enough.

*

My mother would look back from the door when she stood up from scrubbing (always the last thing to do was to scrub your way out) and assess the rightness of it. Perhaps she would go back to move an object, adjust a chair an inch, or wipe a spot on the blinds or lampshade; then she would go back and look again—the aesthetics of making something shine. I believe that image stayed in her mind, as a page of a finished poem stays in mine.

*

Seventy years ago, the year I was born, Richard Wright wrote of being
beaten and abandoned, of his humiliations and tortures in childhood
at the hands of his parents, of his lifelong mental suffering, and how
these experiences fueled his writing. He describes the voices warring
inside him: "In the main we are different from other folk in that, when
an impulse moves us, when we are caught in the throes of inspiration,
when we are moved to better our lot, we do not ask ourselves: 'Can we
do it?' but: 'Will they let us do it?' Before we black folk can move, we
must first look into the white man's mind to see what is there, to see
what he is thinking, and the white man's mind is a mind that is always
changing." I think of the lessons my father taught me. He was born ten
years after Wright's birth, his violent and handsome mother brought
up in the Colored Children's Industrial Home; his grandmother, born
shortly after slavery. How many generations does it take to undo
history?

*

When I knew I would not "get well," that I would never be the girl my
parents wanted, that no matter how much therapy I did and how many
books I wrote, I was stuck with myself, that I had to accept my past
and live with it; then I knew my parents' struggles. They too battled
demons that they couldn't make go away, no matter how much they
suffered, no matter what they did or said, no matter how much they
wanted to love me and be good.

*

Then I gave them credit for what they did right, for what they
accomplished: the weekly salary, the food on the table, the beauty of
face, for understanding the contours of delicacy, of speech; and for the
inner strength: the piercing gray-green eyes that saw good and evil,
the gravedigger's determination and necessity.

*

Then, too, I realized that my fear, that knee-jerk response, has a twin,
an aspect that arises from the same infant sprout: the part that forgets
sorrow and is out in the world playing, that notices the first gold light
lying on the airy branches of the willow in spring—an image that
comes unbidden.

*

There is a picture of my father holding me when I was just a few
months old. We are standing in front of the bungalow my family
shared with my aunt and uncle until I was seven. Above my father's
head, you can see the window in the one large finished area of the attic
where we lived, a door and thin wall away from bare wood beams and
summer's blistering heat. I don't remember why someone snapped
us; perhaps it was a celebration—my mother's birthday was in July, I
would have been four months old—my father is in a casual shirt with
open collar and plain pants, a working man's clothes. There we are
in that first public document: I with a look of obvious discomfort,
perhaps even the smugness of a little judge; and he looking off-
balance, as if someone had just thrown him a bundle of snakes. He
doesn't know what to do with me. What part of himself does he not
know how to hold? My lips are sealed, almost puckered in displeasure.
I am either not yet afraid to show my feelings, or else the very brain
doesn't know enough yet to hide me. He too looks inexperienced; in
tenderness and violence, he is a novice, a beginner, a baby.

*

Once in a dream I saw my father as a pasty white dog, starved,
ignorant, graceless; I said to myself, that is what evil looks like. As
I grew stronger, my father grew weaker, until a frightened boy lived
inside me. "Rest here now safe near your daughter." In bringing myself
forth, I had become his protector.

*

the poem is change
the poem in change
the end of the poem is change
to change in the poem
to change by the poem
to hold the change
in the poem
to be changed by the poem
(the poem is change)
to change by writing the poem
(the writing is change)
to hold the change in the writing
to hold the change by writing
to breathe through the change
to write through the change
to breathe by writing
to write by breathing
to change by breathing
the change is breathing
to hold the breath
to hold the writing
to hold the change
to hold it

& let it go.

ACKNOWLEDGMENTS

Grateful acknowledgment is made to the following publications, in which poems in this book were previously published.

American Poetry Review ("my dad & sardines," "Sunday Afternoon at Claire Carlyle's," and "To a cruel lover"); *Callaloo* ("Dolls" and "When the goddess makes love to me"); *Creative Nonfiction* ("Burial sites," under the title "Beds"); *5 AM* no. 34 ("The iris and chicken fat," "A little prayer to our lady," "Untitled," and "When I touched her"); *On the Issues: The Progressive Women's Magazine* and Poetrybay.com ("On a picture of the Buddhist monk Pema Chödrön"); *Ploughshares* ("For my unnamed brother [1943–1943]); *Prairie Schooner* ("Another poem of a small grieving for my fish Telly," "Gershwin," "On the reasons I loved Telly the fish," "Special ears," and "The undertaker's daughter"); *Rattle* ("For Telly the fish").

"Burial sites" (under the title "Beds") was also published in *Best American Essays* (2011).

"The night I stopped singing like Billie Holiday" was published in *Shaping Memories: Reflections of African American Women Writers* (2009).

I would like to thank the John Simon Guggenheim Memorial Foundation for a fellowship that allowed me to write many of these poems. I would also like to thank the Rockefeller Foundation for a residency at the Bellagio Center; and the Corporation of Yaddo, Virginia Center for the Arts, the UCross Foundation, and Henry Reese and Diane Samuels for providing me with space and time.

Thanks to Ellen Bass, Lucille Clifton, Tony Derricotte, Lynn Emanuel, Terrance Hayes, Lisa Johnson, Nancy Kline, Deborah Golden Meade, Eryn Morgan, Jeff Oaks, Sharon Olds, Alicia Ostriker, Sonia Sanchez, Ellen Smith, Judith Vollmer, and Ann Walston for your loving critiques of this book. Thanks to all the Cave Canem family for the years of love and support.

My heartfelt thanks, as well, to Brian Weller, Alison Meyers, Cornelius Eady, Sarah Micklem, Carolyn Micklem, Francis Gargani, Diane Mazefsky, and Susan Wind.

Special thanks to Ed Ochester for his support of my work over the years and for the Pitt Poetry Series.